Parto Plants a Seed

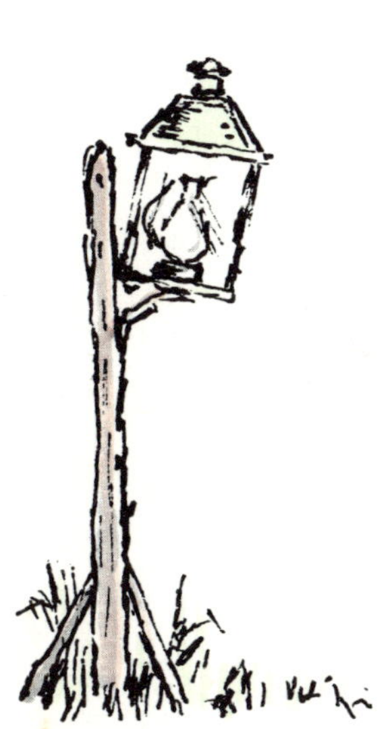

by Ben Shecter

PAN BOOKS LTD · LONDON

for little Eric

Partouche lived in Madame Gounard's backyard.
There he passed his time chatting with Raymond the fieldmouse,
and being scolded by Madame for munching her vegetables.

Madame would shake her finger and cry at the top of her voice, "Partouche, you must not munch the vegetables!"

But he loved vegetables, especially corn.
When he was scolded he wished he had a garden all his own.

One day Partouche discovered a leftover seed in the greenhouse.
He planted the seed in the railway yard
near the house of the stationmaster.

When Madame was busy, Partouche would sneak out of the garden and visit his seed. He carried with him Madame's rusty old watering can.

And he wore a pair of Madame's old gardening gloves.

This made him feel like a real gardener.

One morning he noticed a green sprout. The seed was beginning to grow.

That afternoon Raymond stopped by to chat.
Partouche told him all about his little plant.
"Come. I will show it to you," said Partouche.
He opened the garden gate and ran towards the railway yard.

T-O-O-T, T-O-O-O-T! the train whistle warned.

"Partouche!" Raymond shouted. "Be careful of the train!"

Partouche jumped out of the path of the big engine and ran into the yard. Raymond followed close behind.

"Partouche, you have planted your corn in with Monsieur Fouvais's geraniums."
Partouche looked closely at his plant. "Really? Is it corn? How wonderful!"

"Monsieur Fouvais will not think it is so wonderful," cautioned Raymond. "Why didn't you plant your corn in Madame Gounard's garden?"

"I did not even ask her," said Partouche. "I know she would not let me."

For many days Partouche carefully tended his corn.
The stalk was beginning to grow tall.

One morning as Partouche was weeding he was interrupted. "Partouche!" cried Raymond. "The stationmaster!"

Monsieur Fouvais suddenly leaped out from behind the washing.
"And what are you doing in my flower bed?"
He charged towards them with a sheet caught in his braces,
and stumbled.

"We must rescue the corn!" commanded Partouche.
While Monsieur Fouvais was freeing himself from the sheet
Raymond laughed. "His face is redder than all the geraniums."
Partouche and Raymond carried the cornstalk behind a large coal bin.

"We will plant it here," whispered Partouche,
"hidden away from the angry stationmaster!"
"Maybe it would be better to plant it in Madame Gounard's garden."
"No," said Partouche. "I am sure she would scold me."

The next day the cornstalk was bending low to the ground.
Sounding like a wise old plant doctor, Raymond said,
"Without the sun the plant will get sick and die."
Partouche nodded. "That is true."

Partouche and Raymond sat on a log and thought.

"We will have to plant it somewhere else," sighed Partouche.

The sun was shining brightly in a corner of the railway yard.
"There's a good spot!" shouted Partouche.
"Madame's garden is a better spot," answered Raymond.
But Partouche wouldn't listen and planted the cornstalk once again.

He was happy when it straightened in the sunshine.

But Raymond sadly shook his head.

"Partouche, you have planted your corn in the middle of the railway line."

C-H-U-G, C-H-U-G, T-O-O-T, T-O-O-O-T!

Partouche clung desperately to his cornstalk.
"The train will be on top of us soon," pleaded Raymond.
The big engine moved closer. The engine-driver waved his arms.

THULMP, s-c-r-e-e-c-h, BAM! The train stopped. "What do you call this?" shouted the engine-driver. "This is a case for the authorities!" He went to call them.

The authorities arrived looking very important.
They examined the cornstalk and then began to mutter.
Finally, the most important authority spoke.

"Who planted this corn?"

The engineer said, "He did!"

The authority put on his spectacles and looked at Partouche.

Then all the authorities spoke among themselves again.
Their voices got louder and louder and LOUDER, until everyone was shouting.
"Cut it down!" one of them yelled.

While the men continued to argue, Raymond whispered to Partouche, "Let us bring the cornstalk to Madame Gounard's garden."

"But what will Madame say?"

"Wait and see," were Raymond's words of advice.

Partouche and Raymond carried the cornstalk to Madame's backyard. "Partouche," said Madame Gounard. "What a beautiful cornstalk." "Thank you," said Partouche. "May I plant it in your garden?"

"Why, of course," said Madame.
"I would be pleased to have the cornstalk in my garden."
It grew and grew because Partouche took good care of it.
Raymond helped also.

One day late in summer Madame, Partouche, and Raymond went on a picnic.
Madame brought a blanket. Raymond brought some salt.
Partouche brought ears of corn from his plant for everyone.
And they all munched together under the trees.